*Ha Ha*

*Also by Andrew Jordan:*

St Catherine's Buried Chapel (Taxus, 1987)
The Mute Bride (Stride, 1998)

# Andrew Jordan

## Ha Ha

Shearsman Books
Exeter

First published in in the United Kingdom in 2007 by
Shearsman Books Ltd
58 Velwell Road
Exeter EX4 4LD

www.shearsman.com

ISBN-13  978-1-905700-12-7

ISBN-10  1-905700-12-1

Copyright © Andrew Jordan, 2007.

The right of Andrew Jordan to be identified as the author of this work has been asserted by him in accordance with the Copyrights, Designs and Patents Act of 1988. All rights reserved. No part of this publication may be reproduced, stored in a retrieval system, transmitted in any form or by any means, electronic, mechanical, photocopying, recording or otherwise, without the prior permission of the publisher.

Some parts of this book have previously appeared, or will appear, in *Angel Exhaust, Eratica, Fire, Oasis, PN Review, Shearsman, Stand, Tabla*. 'Looking Down' was commissioned by Southern Arts for BBC South's 'ArtsWeek' promotion (1998).

Cover design by Andrew Jordan.

The publisher gratefully acknowledges financial assistance from
Arts Council England.

# Contents

| | |
|---|---|
| Giggle | 7 |

*Part One: In Outline*

| | |
|---|---|
| The Martyrs | 11 |
| Idealisation | 12 |
| Sovereignty | 13 |
| The Antiquarians | 14 |
| Form | 17 |
| The Scouring | 18 |
| The Plagiarist | 19 |
| Palimpsest | 21 |
| Weightlessness | 23 |
| The Plumpton Cross | 25 |
| Neither Matter Nor Spirit | 26 |
| The Marker | 28 |

*Part Two: Mythopoeia*

| | |
|---|---|
| Advent | 35 |
| Amnesia | 38 |
| Tricorn | 39 |
| On Bevois Mount | 40 |
| In Transference | 41 |
| Near Houndwell Park | 42 |
| Near Danebury Ring | 43 |
| Looking Down | 46 |
| Near Lomer Farm | 47 |
| On Days Off | 49 |
| The Fovant Badges | 50 |
| The Crown | 53 |
| Homelands | 54 |

*Part Three: Wessex*

| | |
|---|---|
| Broadcast | 61 |
| White Horse | 63 |
| The I | 64 |
| Georgics | 66 |
| The Long Barrow | 68 |
| On Hilda's Low | 69 |
| Wessex | 70 |
| Tuning In | 72 |
| Echo and Edgelessness | 74 |
| In Dull November | 75 |
| Thanksgiving | 76 |
| A Southampton Stone Circle | 78 |

*Part Four: The Source*

| | |
|---|---|
| Ha Ha | 83 |

# Giggle

The lynchet shook, as if with laughter.
      He had said
that from the tump –
      looking west,
below the azimuth,
      at the equinox –
we would see
      a holy script
edged into place
      by shadows and light.
We saw words
      greeked into words,
the first text always
      obscured by the rest.
*"...and all interpretations*
      *became, to us,*
*just territory – something lost*
      *we were not free of."*
Gestalt. Metaview.
      The last ditch
really spelling it out
      for you – *"She is gone"* –
and that field caught
      in an image
of lit leaves.
      We freed up
those ludic texts
      of hillscape, rising
into an ideal.
      There is no way back
onto those hills.
      Look from the same tump,
along the same alignment,
      at midsummer

and you can see,
  quite clearly,
one word, repeated,
  on every inch
of the placed ground:

  "Ha Ha
Ha Ha
  Ha Ha
Ha Ha."


  He said,

"these places
  are taking
the piss
  out of us."

# Part One: In Outline

# The Martyrs

They hang on crosses
like purple berries
full of our juice. We

are exhausted by martyrs
who smile like vampires
above our heads. "Come

down," we say, "come down,"
but they do not hear,
"we need to eat you."

"You have everything, you talk
madly with the gods,
all at our expense."

They are ever smiling
at some lost point
on the horizon. Or are they

laughing at us, the ones
they have exploited,
lauded and betrayed?

# Idealisation

The high moors swung above the sea
like a piece of landscape placed on stilts
or a scaffolding of light, half come adrift,
that had found its own salvation in the bees
whose tiny wings kept distance in the air
so long as all the heather was in place
(their silver wings, together, anchoring
a form of summer light found nowhere else).
And so it happened, matter was transformed
and landscape drifted high above the sea.

# Sovereignty

On the map, an incomplete description.
A site at the edge of an objective view
of past events. Beyond our jurisdiction,
some chalk digging. Too many theories
tested here; and the emblem of Britain
as Israel is raised where the Ark rests on
pinions of air; the geometry marked by
a thorn tree, an exposure to light.
*Above the spectral farm, a spectral field.*
A circle drawn on a block, as if etched
into a square and the failed earthwork,
suggesting; 'an eternity'; an action chasing an outcome;
a deferred completion (she *was* already late);
a monument, difficult to detect.

# The Antiquarians

## 1 *The Reconstructionists*

They'd meet at intervals to explore
a narrative, a rumour, an ideology;
passing through an ancient system of symbols,
they climbed to the high field –
praying in the shadowed Roman ditch –
to map the tunnel entrances.
They talked of ancient graffiti, the image
of the horse, of Ireland crucified and –
in the rarefied, pre-dawn aura of success –
the buried armouries they'd find.
They'd keep place as place, cleansed of placelessness,
and make the low, post-English hills
a Hades of the placeless world, seeing
a newly fleshed-out view, shining,
that called for Eve, renewed by death,
to rise out of the grave again – her hair
shocked white by sin – her heart
so broken with remorse that she'd do anything
to be pitied and then killed again.

## 2  Heritage, Southampton

Someone was executed near the reservoir.
That's good. Near the A33.
A butler killed for stealing *plate*. His soul
is trapped in water, slippery, like
a pale organ, shot from the skin,
dropped by butter fingers into place.
Meanwhile, in Lord's Wood, archaeologists
dig banks and ditches that did not
exist before they came to make
a cold, prosthetic history. Quaint,
how they make the ground look old.
The *Cutted Thorn* beside the road
seems a place of ritual, ancient,
instead of something just made up,
a history that we'd believe.

## 3  Kore

I sang the field edge, bloody minded,
lyrical – the nameless row of cottages
along from the silos, the grain depot.
I saw my father, my fracturing,
in the distance with a gun, walking
out of first light – a clear remembering –
with a pheasant in his hand, for us.
I found a schoolgirl in a ditch, fainting,
a lost cross country runner to revive.
Her earthen body had attracted me
to the hedge, where she painted her lips
with a rain-wet blackberry, strangely.
She liked to see herself as innocent
and, as a symbol, she overwhelmed the loss
of place in me by grounding it in flesh;
but then, as symbol, place was held by her
until she too was locked inside a myth.

# Form

It would seem black, from a distance,
if it were not silvered in air; some
forged artefact lifted on a wedge of light.
A filtered upland, it held an idea –
or seemed to – that altered as you looked at it;
a chalice, like a cornucopia, all embossed;
a glossary of antique signs; one concept
aligned with another, becoming protean.
The source of hope, you might say, responding
to an image in the air, something inspired.
My idea of an echo of a form.
It filled me and it emptied me at once.

# The Scouring

The graven image
on the hill is fading now.
A chalk cut image
"in outline only"

lost under hawthorn.
*Nothing is known
of this figure.* Seen
only when the light

is at an angle, it hides within
our consciousness;
a memory to share
called 'blossom'.

*A depression revealed.*
An anchored light
or antique sign,
drawn into consciousness.

So I walked onto it,
as if to ditch
the outline of a self
from this tradition.

# The Plagiarist

## 1 *Topiary Landscapes*

I watched as the slope grew steeper and the yews
grew darker above the farm, and the turf –
within the distance you'd denied –
appeared to me as precious, in description.
The synthesis remains there mystified,
its artifice, a real ground, concealed
within the countryside that we'd invented –
its unedged fields, a land raised up on stilts,
its imaged settlements, so picturesque –
which you would claim is local and authentic.


## 2 *Minstrelsy (In the Frame)*

Between the beginning and the far edge, under
the lipped ridge, the village sits. Almost authentic –
a small and displaced product of the land –
rebirthed, fenced. So real, so muted and very well connected.
Everything we said seemed to be scripted,
and all our thoughts about that were repressed,
until we were forgetful of the story
and thought each other known, the village rooted.


## 3 *Authentic Poem*

The landscape tilted under clouds, into separateness.
You told how absences hold up the trees, their
impossible branches leaning heavily on our yearning
for a word that is authentic, a patch of ground.
My symbol in the slope – unknown within relationship,
not socialised and so not made – is a character, distinctive now.

"...*on the tip of my tongue.*" See how imperfect our
most prized possessions are, how we are unable
to pull off sincerity, real authorship, or clarity?
There's no grand gesture, even resignation is false.


## 4  In Effect

Were I to whisper into this false dawn –
send my words into each other, slip them between
the misted boughs, into the leaf mould, the mirage
that an ancient slope describes – you'd hear me.
There'd be nothing descriptive, and I'd be guarded,
knowing you were there, all ears, eager to know.
There have been too many feet on these hills
to see them as ideal; too many descriptions, events.
We stand in abstraction – the essence – the alphabet of things,
and make of this a context for the meanings
we have to walk away from to perceive.

## Palimpsest

*"...on our field trip we found giant letters concealed in the landscape. Huge forms edged by footpath and motorway, the ditched and banked council estate. A text of place, a knowledge in the field edged with pylons."*
— Dr Charles Mintern

1

She wore the mantle of
the real world: Utopia, masked
and wrapped up in wounds,
a myth of repression.

"...walking along her edged field,
pulling serifed trees
from out of the view
easily for her,

and she'd do the distances
as if they were real."
*There's no way to recall
what can't affect you.*

2

Was she blessed
or merely brain damaged? How she
read the holy script
of the edged embankment,

recovering
whole sequences of words
from scenery.
"It's hysteria," she said,

*"before it was seen."*
(And all based on
an image of
herself as her daughter.)

3

She stood beside
the letter N
at the base of
the airless motte,

then walked to
the strange font
of a massive A
stretched out below:

"It's all a part
of *nature*," she said,
laughing at
the way the land

could still describe
the after glow
of the time God spoke
the word she'd read.

# Weightlessness

## 1 *Atmosphere*

We walked to the copse across the high dome of the field
to see how feeling – rooted in abstraction –
deepened as we climbed. The trees
swayed above the field – the valley already
deep in gloom – and we looked on the landscape in delight
as if it underpinned identity
and the top of Knowle Hill, the black wood,
grew atmospheric as the shadows lengthened.

## 2 *Situation*

These ancient barrows, placed bureaucracies,
are forged within a myth of nationhood,
enclosed within the chancel of the state,
its mysteries, its theatre and its map.
You'd glimpse a spectral city through the trees,
its golden towers raised by holy kings –
their mythed ascendancies – echoing Troy,
their living and the wonder of their cost,
their mythic legions and cathedral walls, perfected,
before you'd know that this, to you, is loss.

## 3 *Defection*

Since you saw the hill destroyed and found a self
loosed by the mud slide, unmade and unplaced,
you have loved unknitted soil, trees on their sides,
and the burst earthwork, released and shifting.
The JCBs that work the risen slope
seed old places with new forms that we
might take the strain of being on our backs
and see a nameless ground, a clarity.

## 4 Ontology

The ground we walk upon is strange to us –
we've grown unsure of it, and what it means –
as if we'd slept and, waking, couldn't grasp
a commonplace we'd shared within a dream.
It's strange, that we perceive no edge of self –
no boundary stone, old stump of ancient cross,
no infilled ditches and no ploughed out mounds –
to place us, like an object, on the ground
in any way we might be conscious of.

## The Plumpton Cross

I want to visit the Plumpton Cross again,
*"now almost obliterated."* It was of the Greek type,
two hundred feet across, placed on the high downs,
disrupting the view. How it must have created
diversions in its time – giving the eye something
to linger on, an anomaly. There is no evidence
of this turf cut feature now, nor of its meaning
beyond the myths of place that place provides,
of battles and of Kings, ambitions lost, old tales
that light the trees and lift the earth
with a feeling that is palpable and known,
that we'd feel again as authenticity, as *sensed*,
when – within feeling – it is only myth,
the very thing this feature once displaced
in how it showed itself as real amongst
the textures of its own synthetic ground.

## Neither Matter Nor Spirit

1
In one corner, a tree
edged with petals.
A stump of wall.
A track through nettles.
Things I invented.

An echoing valley
and the abstract dead,
the old geometry
in what you said,
and what I made of it.


2
The moat that edged
the ground is grown
full of weeds, a silting up
has seen to that.
*Garlanded.* A May wreath.

The things we see
remain concealed
in what is said, our
imagery, and we become
distant and indefinite.


3
As if known I stood
beside the sunlit tree
before the ruin.
I stood in, as if to be
an aspect of

a perfect realm,
the lost design
of what belongs,
and what it means,
identity.

# The Marker

*The safety of this ancient fort brings with it profound isolation. This leads to desire and a closeness with the object...*
— Mintern, *The Transference Relationship*

### 1 Under Castle Corbenic

Above us, the camp on its height.
A cruelty or "controlling behaviour, ditched and banked,"
which functions by diverting her away. *A complex.*
He drew an arc – over Unity – making "places of safety"
she could put her image in, for her re-membering.
*An isolation or neurosis built of earth.*
They stood amongst the columns of the dead, 'taking in'
the blossom by the sluice, "the lyric I locate in her"
or "the white display of the spirit in early spring."


### 2 A Moral Compass

It was a circular earthwork, representing a "viscous cycle,"
the Guide said. *All crumpled in.* "We will start at Low Self-Esteem
and walk to Relief through Sexual Fantasy and Masturbation..."
*A sense of being.* "...then into Eye-Contact, Abuse and
Rejection and on into Annihilation and Narcissistic Withdrawal."
A thick drift of parsley filling the ditch
on either side. The track you skipped along,
as if to let me know that it was *your* heart
that made the world so light, *your* self
in blossom – like a victim – at the gate.


### 3 Her Innocence

A tumulus or tumour in the ground; a lump
indicating a memory and retaining it as a feature, "rich in history,

antique and mysterious..." *A promise broken here.*
She moved from spire to spire across the land
and revelled in the 'gothic' and the 'calm' –
applying 'spiritual' to control – and taking in
Temple, Mosque and Holy Mound. The core complex –
or *how she has been sexualised* – processed on the line
from Loathing to the Absolute.

### 4 In the Sculpture Garden

In the park, the art of immanence. Her block before her.
*A cube.* A spiritual pattern in the lawn,
solidified; an inversion or potential in the maze;
under topiary, an abstract of Hell. A *compulsion* or
"alignments in all things." It is Unity,
comfort, a known way of life; it is the self
she comes home to. "...*a modern work.*"
Below the Mansion of Beyond, she withdrew
into the shade of an exhibit of the soul.

### 5 The Pilot

She climbed the fuselage of the long barrow, calling out:
"...it's the crashed craft of a Priest or King..."
> *She walked the length of it.*

The pilot, in his crown of thorns, below – crouched
at the controls – was working the machinery of water.
Sluice and spring. His skin, "a bleached flower."
*I heard her calling.* She was in alignment with the sun
and I looked up – along her shadow – at the source.
*Blinding.* A lens or neurone receiver, flared;
the edge of a sphere, broadcast from within.
*She stood above him in the flesh.* "I'm over the cockpit now,"
> she said.

## 6  Over Matriarchs

We walked to the edge of the trench. *She'll be disappointed*
*if I don't come this way again.* The alder, splayed
from its root, in a radiance. *"Stripped down to the mechanism."*
An ambulatory incline below the church, still working.
Images of the beast, barely visible now, in the lifted head
of the nettle, redeeming. *An arrangement or stronghold.*
Maternal in aspect, the way down into death, an
"obsolete vallum", high over elder, we might sit within.
*An incubation.* A process of resurrection. A social effect, seen in:

1. A tilted tree, compensated for.
2. An altered water-course, leading to "silting up."
3. *An unforeseen affect or flood.*
4. A pilgrimage into "sublimation."
5. A fulfilment, expressed as 'ritual'.
6. *The transference in this.*
7. A love, weighed against higher things.
8. The white horse, sleeping on the slope, which we saw move.
9. A tradition.

"I think it's Neo-Platonist," she said.

## 7 What she said

From within the fortress – amongst twisted oaks,
    romantically inclined –
she called down. "It's a functioning emblem..."
Then, turning away, "there's no need to apologise."
*That's good.* On higher ground, above enshrouded willow,
they formed a line and stood at either end,
with nothing between them.
"...it is a journey out of love and into death."
*A pilgrimage.* See how the boughs part. *"To walk that line..."*
She stood by Hawthorne in the dusk, "a splendour woven
by the eye," to emphasise the distances between
one fort and another.


## 8 The Spiral

We walked the spiral, or where it had been, going through
each part of the complex – over and over – and faster until
things inside were clarified;
and the world – always shifting back, against the sun –
lagged behind the consciousness
"ripe with giddy innocence"
created from our dancing in
an image from Antiquity.


## 9 Open Day Over

There was a light behind the hedge beside the path
placed to lead the lost on their way home
over dead-nettles, into an ideal called 'nectar'.
She dropped an imperfect flower, off-white and tainted;

not pristine, nor with meaning, but for me.
Something dusted with pollen, below depth
(the garden, convulsing around her, "in spasm").
I took it as a keepsake, when she discarded it.
*Those torn petals.* The pattern she extended into me.

## Part Two: Mythopoeia

# Advent

1. A royal hunting lodge – antlers
   wedged on the paling – old skulls on stakes
   at the gate – the leaves burning.

2. A dead king naked in the arms
   of his stolen empress. Murdered, again,
   in a wet summer by the men of leaves.

3. Those men in autumn – their faces
   a brittle mess (each curling leaf on their bodies
   revealing an eye beneath).

4. You, half-naked, climbing from a well.
   You had been unfaithful and were
   carrying the dead king's child.

5. A holy angel, captured at the gate,
   staked out and dismembered,
   its voice box removed, still singing.

6. A clump of mistletoe falling
   from a cloud. People walking and rewalking
   the causeways, to no effect.

7. One of those times when our heads sprang
   from one body. An angel and a devil
   kissing in the hollow tree.

8. A holy miscarriage – we were sure
   you were pregnant – bloody nausea
   and a star rising, rising, despite us.

9. The site of the lodge, burnt clear
   of all but the bones of the king,
   his good hearted soldiers, the enemy.

10   A careful procession returning
     you to this hill after long years:
     a box carried shoulder high, an absence.

11   One, they open the box. Two, they look
     inside. Three, they gasp in dismay.
     A skeleton, a rotted wedding dress, within.

12   The priest dreamed she pushed up
     the warm earth in spring – fragile flesh
     fresh grown on her cheeks, rosily.

13   She was known to the children as Ana.
     Often they were heard laughing with her,
     but when we looked she had gone.

14   A naked boy, six years old, in the woods –
     freshly strangled – you could still see
     the bruises left by her lips.

15   Five men pulling on a rope, at midnight.
     Slowly the moon iced the mad
     horns of light on the solitary cloud.

16   She stood over him – her dress ripped
     to reveal her genitals. "Suck the spirit,
     Priest," she said, "call me Sheela-na-gig."

17   In the moonlit cathedral the king's bones
     climbed from their chest: he danced with saints,
     a new queen, fresh horns on their heads.

18  They sealed her in a coffin – carried her
    past the siege tower, the lines, and out
    to the parish edge, where she leapt out, alive.

19  I am Mary, she said, I am a coven,
    she said, I am thirteen women in one,
    she said, worship your new Lord.

20  In the valley the carollers sang. We chased
    mummers around the earthwork, trying
    to understand the names of death.

21  They pulled the treasure to the edge
    of the well. "There it is," said one,
    and the rope broke, and it was gone.

22  O holy one, we will not crucify
    either you, or our own desires, or those
    we love, who love us. We promise. *Truly*.

23  She was pregnant, we were sure. Roped
    down, so she could not run, we beat her
    and said, "You will give birth, you will."

24  She had crawled, her own life a brand
    consumed by fire, like a sun. A grain goddess.
    Her holiness ripening corn for the poor.

25  Last year's mutton dressed as lamb. We killed her,
    put the bride in the box, let the queen
    out of town. No worries, Lord, she will return.

# Amnesia

> Between villages, the chalk uplands of
> the Atrebates, polished by industry into
> brilliance. You can sense an ideology – in
> customs and place-names, the slang of
> agricultural contractors, and pub signs –
> a yew tree inheritance. Everything is
> suddenly traditional and old; the vast
> acreage of the field, the combine beating
> the bounds – a characteristic copse – and
> the bench preserved in a state of decay and
> the bus stop, in a holly tree, abandoned.

Somewhere there is mercy you can trust – not
always an isolated house, loosed feathers.

> Home, for her, was a sense of the past,
> though she cannot recall it. A girl struck
> dumb by the Lammas road kill – harvest
> of partridges, some still flapping – in
> amongst the spill of grain. They had gone
> to a nature reserve – for *nature* read *the
> past*. Today we have *environment*, which
> we create, an instant side-effect of how we
> live. The neat gardens and tidy interiors
> suggestive of sexuality controlled or an
> absence of sexuality.

## Tricorn

*"...it is the jewel in Palmerston's crown,
the light at the centre..."*

A cold war cathedral, built to be buried
under a mound, as at Silbury.
Known to the Druids as "Elen's Bower",
it was a May Pole enclosure – in past times –
where maidens danced amongst the stones
of a circle, by the hanging tree, *in hysteria*.
Aubury surveyed this sward, calling it
"the mound ship of Portus, and of his household."
Being aligned with the fort at Hilsea –
and echoing of the Lump Forts in the swell,
and the muniments on Portsdown Hill,
and at their centre, measured easily –
it guards its groves and maidens, although fallen,
and holds the platform of the city up
above the rising waves, unconsciously.

## On Bevois Mount

*A single letter, then another and another. A sense of*
*something underneath the rest, the first word,*
*an Ur-text.*
          Mintern, A *Survey of the Hills of Wessex*

She turned to call the children back to her.
They saw her in the light, against the blue,
as she waited on the footpath to the mound.
There's nothing but alignments for her now,
how one thing leads to another, or how –
faltering – time can seem to stop
with what you said and did just out of reach.
The children, all oblivious, played on.
How many times she'd paced the pattern out.
Gog and Magog – their broken lettering
etched into her memory. *This year, an Easter Rising.*
She thought of things, as images, and tried
to grasp all the abstractions in her mind –
St. Deny's, the Itchen and Osborne Road –
which she had seen, but never understood.
I saw her, from a distance, looking down
as if her Sacred Heart – an abstract line –
were printed, like a symbol, in the ground
and all that it might mean, or might deny,
were lost to her, in how she'd slanted it.

# In Transference

*"An ideal in the tower, partially fallen..."*

1

At Bishop's Waltham you described
how stones were all religion once
as if held hostage to the faith
that raised its vaulting in the air,
amongst the trees, to make the song
more beautiful, imprisoned there.
You stood on a causeway, in transference
and empty, a hollow thing
seen in the distance, blossoming.
*Under a wall, on raised ground,*
*the may tree we forced into flower.*


2

You stood in the window, looking out.
Going carefully on the steps, over stitchwort,
you lowered your self onto a ledge.
The ground was printed under you.
You seemed slight, so far up,
looking over the trees to the fields –
which held no image, being unremembered –
then down, at me – a lost consciousness –
climbing to the causeway, all fleshed out,
looking for perspectives you had known
or coming to possess you from below.

## Near Houndwell Park

You watch the park at dusk to feel
the balancing of distances combine
with scaffoldings of cloud, ladders
of light, to reconstruct the evening air
above the trees in their first green –
and the aura of the buses, their scarlet –
and the cherry tree in blossom
beyond them in the park. Invisible,
the workmen have begun to hoist
stars into the sky. The first of them
shines above the avenue of lawns,
the dark disintegration of the self,
as we expand, without boundaries,
freed of all identity that counts.

# Near Danebury Ring

1
Hungry Hill. A fine belt of trees giving shelter to fields.

A long barrow, tapering in plan, under grass.

2
Oval Barrow visible
above level of field,
subject to ploughing.
O.S.A. No. SU33

NW10. Ref: 1.
Site under plough
but ditch visible
on air photographs.

3
Flat topped barrow
situated in a small copse,
surrounded by traces of a ditch.
She has walked

the circle of
the complex again, arriving at
the point of
sexual attraction.

What is lost is felt
in this embrace.
*Down Farm.*
*Lopcombe.*

**4**
A hill fort south-east of Popple Light Copse.
Single bank and ditch in an area of approximately 6 acres.
Mutilated near its eastern end, she felt the
rucked ground. There was abuse by
the remains of an earthwork and she says
it was "partly ploughed out." She stands
further off, visible as crop and soil marks –
a fragile form – in air photographs.


**5**
Barrow (Probable Site),
mutilated in the centre,
where she was harmed,
there is
nothing visible from

the ground. (Comprises two
shapeless contiguous
mounds with a
maximum height of 0.4m.)


**6**
Two ring ditches, apparently confluent, visible as crop marks. Two faint 'bumps' are visible on the modern field path. Barrow (Alleged). *Period Unknown*. She stands over it, feeling a "casting off of valued things." No trace can be found of this barrow. Where life began, a passion at the centre of "two large concentric rings." Something of the future fertilised. *A lesson we must forget*. Behind her, in chronology, the Lost Barrows (2): A. Vague mound 24m. in diameter. B. No trace. A feeling under pasture. She led me on, "but there is no trace to be

found…" No trace of a barrow seen at the above given siting which fails in a pasture field. She has described:

1. A ploughed down bowl barrow. 29.0m. by 26.5m.
2. A stubble field, way off.
3. No traces of a ditch.
4. The chalk ring round the lower part.
5. Romano-British sherds found here May 2nd, 1920.
6. Wonston Manor Farm.
7. Aerial photographs showing detailed plan of settlement.
8. Ditched enclosures.
9. A site now ploughed out / Isle of Wight Hill.

Crop mark of large concentric double-ditched enclosure and other marks. She gave up on her sovereignty for "a closeness with the object" and walked in Loathing afterwards.

(Completely destroyed, but flints visible
after ploughing.)

# Looking Down

*"...ASWE – meaning 'Admiralty Surface Weapons Establishment'
– dominates the skyline over Portsmouth, like a basilica or Kremlin,
shaping the lives of those below..."*

"It's five o'clock, by the shadows on the hill,"
you said, crouching to look
at *viper's bugloss*. A strange light over the harbour.
We were under ASWE, a weapons establishment
we had been advised to avoid:
sight lines converging on the main gate from
Eastney and St. Mary's. "A prominent secret."
*Tunnels connect it to a chapel at Southwick –
they say – and a Motte and Bailey, a long barrow.*
From a centre of conspiracy, you looked down
to watch me as I walked below – my image
broken in the glare – as if you did not know me or
had never thought, before, of what was there.

"We are all connected now," I said.

# Near Lomer Farm

### 1 Exterior

In the copse you laughed at me,
holding up a leaf
as something representative
of a complex, repression.

*"Anything will do..."*
Your body emblematic –
you cupped your hands
in your lap, a pool of light –

revealing an anxiety.
*A centring.* That light –
reflected from your face –
illuminating everything;

the matter of my soul, beyond the trees,
in an abstract field;
the form and mask
I wear, my sympathy.

### 2 Interior

Off on your own, you sat down
in a domestic enclosure,
clasping your arms
against the complex.

*Something to withdraw from,
this settlement.*
"A gesture or habit
to measure distance by."

A little used path,
faint in the grass, leading from
consciousness
into the body. A depression

which, as it is defined,
implies a connection –
no matter how concealed –
between outer and inner.

## On Days Off

They will drive down the shrouded lane – their 'tunnel of remembered light' – to lay-by or car park, the gritted pull-in. They will see emblazoned hills and sense the sprung steel in the downs – a cantilevered span, poised and fluid – a prospect balanced on infinity. They will hum to the dead, below ground – who will climb to them through roots, old cables, the hidden pipes and vents – and feel the things of nature to be real.

> Nothing is lost.
> Even innocence
> has been conserved.
> A notice board
>
> on a hill,
> under angled light,
> a depth of shadow.
> *Anchorage.*
>
> An experience
> simplified
> for someone,
> *not us*, the public.
>
> Easy to read,
> this landscape,
> our ABC
> of history, the state.

They walk their circuits easily, climbing the stile and the field edge, looking over autumn at the patterns in their lives. Love-too-much ghosts. The broken children. They sing on, then, regardless, in their hearts, and turn to find the way back to their cars.

## The Fovant Badges

First, the London Rifle Brigade – 150 feet high.
A regimental crest carved on the downs.

Then the others.

The regiments emblazoned. A tattoo
on high – a mark or a scar to lift the spirits –
or a democratic monument. A battery
of souls gathered
in their potency above this
distance they gazed into.

Sweet light of early morning – a pale light
to underpin a horror –
or a game to pass the time. *A clock drawn on the downs?*

This reminder of chivalry – a sceptred badge,
a lantern of oak leaves – the work of giants.
An occult history, a white hart in a collar and Mercury,
moving like a ripple in the turf.

In a landscape of antiquities,
these badges are like blossom.

Where pain is, a point of pilgrimage.
Caught in the spectre of an image,

a wound that is renewed by scouring. Near Chislebury Camp –
faint marks on the downs
where armies camped before embarking. Grim's ditch
was built by Odin, they said giants walked this land
before Troy fell, before Brutus.

Somewhere there are graves, they left their dead.
In this ground – vast bones
of a memory – an ancient belief based on
a knowledge of the moon whose light they trapped
in the sphere of a badge, a sliver of light
on the horizon.

Once there were twenty or more, but their light faded.
Colossus of the modern world – lost
regiments – then there were twelve.

Which we can still see, though some have almost perished.

I walked out one day to see the thirteenth,
which appears in dreams. The last full moon of the year.
To Yeats, the thirteenth gyre was totality, a sphere.
In that mysterious centre
the moment is ever new, a light. Still earthed,

Arthur's twelve knights – where
some are not at their best –
at their most beautiful
in their bewildered youth,

in how we have experienced
this frailty at the heart of the self.

Partly grassed over, the ideology
of ordinary men.

There was a regiment for each apostle,
marching from the Summerland into an ideal
or the branch of mythology called Death.

Ranged from east to west, at the equinox
they tell the story of the crucifixion
in tableaux, one for each hour of the day.

The zodiac of the machine age, in which
individuals were absorbed into their sign,
becoming typical, predictable and blessed.
Of the twelve luminous doors –

>	the ways into the moon –
>	some are forever closed.

>	Mars walks balefully
>	over my lover. Venus
>	is a drop of light.

Beneath the monumental names of wars,

soft flesh, tender flesh

that will never again be bruised.

## The Crown

We'd made a crown of snow
the day before and left it
to thaw into the ground,

but a final, bitter frost
contained its frailty, drew out
a hidden jewellery,

and we acknowledged it.
We placed it on her head,
your girl, ten years pure;

and the virgin was made
an exile in her garden.
She stood quite still beneath

the frosty, sterile boughs
of the apple tree.
Some objects become magical,

exclusive and excluded.
The frozen crown possessed
and contained her sense

of who she might have been.
You held up a mirror
and she saw for herself

a grandeur, an isolation;
the power and distraction
in the surfaces of things.

# Homelands

*"Absurd, outrageous and fantastic symbols were splashed across
the fields, like hieroglyphs or headlines, they took away our sense
of self, our power – or our myth of it..."*

1

The edge of the lino was the horned lip of the world:
a thumb-nail, lately hit with a brick, lifting
over concrete, flaky to the touch. Palimpsest of
the kitchen floor – a place of danger: home
of legend – portal to an underworld
where earwigs, mercurial silverfish, moved between
the modern world and this, our realm of myth.


2

I ran in the spin drift, through a countryside,
to a dump in the waste ground: under
corrugated iron we saw half-timbered tunnels,
the white roots of bindweed, underworld grasses.
*A rumour of rats.* A place of resurrection. Home
of some Anglian king – my dream of his daughter
peeling back the bark of the rowan, speaking
tongues of leaves in the cutting, holding
the open door of the next day – bunched
and unripe berries, a bloodied future – saying, *"summer"*.


3

The moon had risen over darkening woods.
She drew the outline of an antique font
on the gate above the weir – as if to image
ownership – and kicked the silvery brooch of dew
from a tuft of grass, leaving it robbed and bruised.
Those heavy Norfolk soils, a marl of autumn,
held her to the bunker in the hedge

which – rooted in the ground, built to withstand
the echoing of some lost, mythic war – balanced
the moon with its silvery evanescence.
I looked into her pale, disked face – its magic –
which was already taken, upon which men had walked.


4
*"This is not home,"* she said, beside the tunnel
under the blackthorn, where the dog had gone.
You cut yourself badly on the fence, and then knew
how alien those fields were – how the horizon
pulled you away from where you were meant to be.
Hours of walking – the flatlands, an undulation.
He went into the tunnel and was lost. Years later,
under Trunch, they heard his dog barking – some
subterranean Black Shuck, a threatened return,
the warriors slaughtering the calf, Dad lifting out
a cradle of guts to be buried. *"Soon you'll be doing this."*


5
It was winter and he realised that, in Norfolk,
there's nowhere to hide from the open night sky.
Something from space could take you. The
constellations stretched – after long years in abstraction –
and clanked like scaffolding robots over the fields.
The king had been there, lost for centuries; now
he peered in through the window, angrily, seeking
information on his daughter – as if scenting her.
Who had she been with? Where going? What had she done?

6
At the base of the slope, behind banked nettles,
we found the maker's mark. A half risen sun,
an empty disk, a tight spiral – a later initial
scratched over this, ER. *"The gateway to my heart."*
One touch of flesh through the front of the dress
was a week's haunting: they were foreign, they had
come to stay, telling us *"...this place is just like home."*
I mouthed the names of places I'd not seen –
Swafham, Castle Acre, Sandringham – and felt the horror
of their occupation. We stood outside the gate, but didn't wave:
*"you speak,"* she said, *"I'm not much good at this."*


7
The copse was manufactured, poised and placed
in perspective, like a fortress in the field. *So self contained.*
It must conceal a grail, a corpse, her face. Two
creeping knights, heroes of the Somme, bane
of the Japanese, kin of the Krays – heirs to this,
a strangeness and a name – we waded through brambles
into *Perilous*. Waist deep. You panicked and you could not run,
falling to the blows, a premonition and the curse
of a pride you had to service all your life.
*She was insubstantial, a tripped figure, fainting away.*


8
As you spoke the stragglers of the hunt
cantered from the park, toward the field.
It was an apple scented feeling – a haunting
of the skin – and we leapt the ditch,
feeling the underworld to be like this – well planned
and laid out – veined with watery cracks. We heard
the first owl calling further on, by Golden Gates,

some pre-linguistic voice, speaking in shapes
of trees, in ground and this, its echoing,
not even using thoughts of us, or pictures.


9
The great house, summoned up, has gone away –
its golden chestnuts and its layered cedars,
its long perspectives and its compensations,
its echo of death, its unpaid debts, its views. I'd
made a shield from an old water heater – some
enamelled visor marked 'Valor' – a flame within –
and I saw the barge – the black flags on the lake –
shifting between island and belonging, the heads
of departments, a corporate – placeless – state
and I raised my sword to the sun, already branded,
and I rode my self through named and ancient fields:
*"The ageing on this place is faked,"* she said.

## Part Three: Wessex

## Broadcast

*Three figures, wind-blown and absorbed, stand above a
vast underground installation, an Admiralty munitions
store they say, engineered into the landscape.*

A mast in the foreground. Something raised before
an image of West Dean. The landscape
spread before us like a map, showing
attributes of power, a simplified process. Each burgh,
a microcosm of gridlines, laboured fields;
each pit and track contained within
a particular and enigmatic horizon.

On Dean Hill, a rampart called *secrecy*, an earthwork
at the end of an ancient ditch or hollow-way;
*our lost memories*. The abode of instinct in
a local amnesia, the Faerie of Munitions, where adit
and slope shaft are not represented,
where knights still sleep in their enchanted halls –
emblazoned – awaiting the call, a signal, the flick
of a switch in the room marked 'war'.
A machine to make identity, *well concealed*.

"There's a dragon in this hill." *She whispered it.*

Way below, beyond the railway line, a stygian ditch
and castle mound, locating the message in the past,
erasing all memories of what we saw. *An acceptable loss.*
Motte and chivalry, the manners of command,
and what it is in us that must submit.

                      I now recall that we had gone to see:

(i) an emblem we are part of – reduced
and represented, self-effacing or disguised;

(ii) a view, as typical as any – described as 'misty',
felt as vulnerable;

(iii) a franchised, votive mass – a land laid low,
*a hidden meaning;*

(iv) an idea we might broadcast of the world.

# White Horse

Too modern, the flow of the line (a disturbance),
and barely civilised. *An instinct or emotion you can see.*
At the Blowing Stone, R. Hippisley Cox –
"and it is seldom that one of the beautiful girls
from the cottage is unwilling to instruct the stranger."

A fleeting glimpse of the Uffington Horse –

it recalls sensations not elsewhere described.

In the distance –
loose on a hill – quintessence. An airborne image.
Royal besom, her method of escape – sensual mare.
In this place, evidence of an unconscious process.
The motion of stillness – a local utility –

has yet to arrive, it is
always departing.

# The I

1
The I exists
on a hillside,
half obscured.
It was marked
by hedgerows which

enclosed a way
between them.
Hollow road.
White campion.
*Processional.*


2
An absence there,
I walked out
onto the downs
to see myself
and describe

the character
forgotten there,
and what was lost
away behind
the anchoring.

3
At night a grid
of rising stars
pulled my gaze
along the lane.
In the distance,

clarity –
light climbing
from the I –
always there
in front of me.


4
It went nowhere,
a strange lane,
all overgrown
and ready then
for grubbing out:

a dead end in
an open field,
visible
for miles around, ending
at the horizon.

# Georgics

*1 The Field*

In the field a labourer works
alone, the job is specialised.

He cuts his tractor into a turn
early, for the spraying boom

which leaves a misted glass of air
over the hedgerow at the top.

Though he is trapped and I am trapped
we cannot share a common place

and the living brings him in
pursuit of his unspoken ends

and he gears up to the last
edging of this placeless field.

## 2 The Winnowing

A peasant woman in the hay
is painted flat against a tank

where the camera, focused in,
collapsed distance into light.

The pastoral asserts itself –
she lifts a load of hopeful hay

and is made to seem to be
of the soil – like scenery.

The soldiers watch her, diffident,
and wait their turn for winnowing

unfleshed landscape into form,
to replace pastoral with real.

# The Long Barrow

## 1 *In the Distance*

From the car, we could see the barrow we had thought was lost;
smudged under stubble, the image of our wish.
The faint autumnal light had drained fence post, path and tree,
leaving insubstantial ground, a copse. Beyond it,
under pools of light, a combine lumbered on, still harvesting.
"One absence of identity to be replaced by another."
*A faded mark.* She stood amongst the bales,
becoming 'absence' in the air, to be recalled as 'loss'.


## 2 *The Long Barrow*

Rows of stubble. The abstract spirals of the bales we
    walked between.
*Glare of modernity.* "The ship of Christ," she said, "fallen."
Visible only as a crop mark, those white sails he abandoned,
ploughed in. She paced the shadow of the wreck
as if to understand the engineers
who dislocated substance from the force that measured it –
liberating science from the matter of the land –
leaving a mechanism, buried on the height.

# On Hilda's Low

A long barrow, constructed so as to appear 'ploughed out';
now under arable and low in the ground. A shadow
at morning, seen in glassy light.[1] A plan cast in the field.[2]
*A disturbance.*[3] "It presents the illusion of a structure,
rising in height from W to E." Her mound, worn into
a slightness of form – in essence, "hard to grasp" –
which we must pity and respect, as if we could engage with it.

[1] The survey failed to find the ditch. Solifluction at the end of a narrow ridge of chalk. It lacks identity, an origin, the name only referred to, not used. 43015737. *Not described.*

[2] A natural feature, angled into narrative – as if some unknown history could be revealed – in the interior, with all the thorns in flower and 'the way', an arbitrary line, too briefly open.

[3] An image in the ground. Below behaviour, *the language of the line*, an insignia or ancient scheme. An old morality – designed to image 'harmony' – abandoned in the field.

# Wessex

## 1 *Remembering*

I placed a pebble in your hand, as we walked out to see the flood. A remnant hedgerow. A blurred clump, like soot, in the silvered field. A signature. An abstract pattern. A spirit or ideal etched into an image of the sky. A mirroring. Heaven – seen from an angle, known by its glare – a flared light off the furthest field. *Something we can work towards.* "What other people have…" You held my body in the stone, whilst I looked at the flooded field.

## 2 *My Lover Speaks*

Around rose-hips,
a wrap of ice. Plastic veins
on the scarlet bulb,
a thrombosis.

"As if something
that had been lost
were encountered
in a feeling called *complete*."

A way into forgetfulness, the path
leads off from
the field edge
to these woods,

then moves on.

## 3 Forgetfulness

It's still there in the field, no longer aligned on meaning – except vaguely – not socialised, nor shaping. A rectangular outline in the ground, raised out of an uneven plane, the tussock. A foundation – something to believe in – precisely drawn. An "altar with earthwork" felt nearby. Placed carefully, a forgetfulness, and under a bough, a significance erased. That which was particular became universal, with no human aspect, nor losses to forget.

# Tuning In

## 1 *Landscape*

*Fog in the valley.* The higher land marooned
or held by an acoustic in the air. I looked down
on a lyric or "a row of trees, tilted on a slope."
The lighted copse – like a grove above the road –
transported. *Something exterior becoming interior.*
An object socialised within an image she made.
*"A carousel of leaves, turning in the light."*
We walked along the Roman road, beneath the crafted
anticline, into a clarity. *"...and no edge to the feeling."*
I saw her gazing at a distant spire, mysterious
in the fog, sculpted from air, in a black nest of trees.
She called me back to walk the line – which she knew –
from loneliness into the field below.

## 2 *Self*

She looked over the roundabout, enjoying the presence
of "a circle, visibly in place" and "forms
made of earth" – the raised carriageways – "embracing it."
*An invented place.* The processing plant –
off the slip-road, past the moated tump –
adrift from its function, risen and symbolic.
*The tree she stood beneath, abstracted.*
She walked ahead, descending into mist, speaking of
"a sphere of vision" we would be aware of in the fog.
*A notion of creation.* "We can move beyond the pain,"
she said, pointing over tree tops into *depth*.
So we went on, into Ardour, "a walled purlieu,"
where the earthly pathways and 'the lines' converged.

## 3 Meaning

A path into origins or "a cross marked on the hill,"
which we seek, "where rooks wheeled above..."
We approached the church, rising from its circle,
on harmonic ground. *Layered, stable and light.*
A moment, "like an arch," which we walked through,
sensing the Druid Stones (recumbent by the bridge)
and Abstraction as *the* tradition, linking things.
*God.* My moments with you. "...the replenishing
of matter, within relationship." A world renewed.
*Weird faith.* Her music filling the church, setting
the stones in motion, creating a dynamic in the air
above the spire – where each particle rotates or
"falls back into history" – which I felt at home with.

# Echo and Edgelessness

## 1 *Decomposition*

We climbed the wood to the hollow yew –
where you took pictures, images of me –
and darkness moved along the branches
into evergreen. You threw your voice into the valley,
over the meadow at the back of the church
(a hall of lit columns, roofless),
and we waited in the echoes of the field
as if the words we'd hear might add to ours
and show a narrative that we could follow –
or think of as our own –
and not the other's edgelessness and sorrow.


## 2 *Unconsciousness and Image*

They walked the embankment, following "an alignment,"
they said, though we offered it as "the edge of text,"
as "the lodging of meaning – as an ideal –
in objects, making matter into imagery."
"It is not you, I etched it, so
it's mine," you said. The hill, the castle and the ground –
the yew tree on the rampart and
the undercroft it stands above –
unconscious of their harvesting,
are printed fields, conceived by you.

## In Dull November

He has long since disappeared, that luminescent
giant of spurious scholarship (a compulsion,
sunk in the deepness). A sludge of chalk
on your boots, "sour and sticky with leaves."

The colossus of prehistory – the superstition
I have seen at dusk beneath enormous clouds
calling with his booming voice of death and loss
and sex. *More phoney than actual.* There is an avenue

of trees aligned on the church to forestall the terrors
that linger in an unprotected mind. We'll walk into love,

she said, we'll walk into love through that obscurity,

that misty light – vacuum of an atmosphere –
through which a terrible ancestor moved.
"...and all true tales of him are blotted out..."

We'll trace the origin of any tender glance,

>articulate an innocence
>or the violence of morality,
>or Victory over Death.

# Thanksgiving

*"...that was the tunnel of dead names I saw, memories of a lane in
summer – those creamy umbels I loved, a buzzing..."*

1
That these lowered fields, blurred into a distance,
should placate us – or the raised embankment,
forming a redoubt, propping up the west wall
of the church, its towering infirmity, should ease
our sense of time, in time's regard – is easy
to understand; as in the abstract, so in the held.


2
You slipped the tiny notched petal between
index and forefinger – a last purple flower
in a dampening, a dark autumn – and you climbed
over terraced hillock, the counterscarp, cradling
this self-heal or bugloss in your hand. We stood
at the back of a field of light – the image
meaning more than the form – releasing myth
into those pastoral depths – the rooks, echoing –
and feeling distances in what we saw.


3
We walked to the coppice, a central place
in this field, hung with lights. The rain,
a comforting, drew out the light of atoms
and that grey atmosphere was silvered, lit:
Eve, now maturing, not a girl, looked back –
astounded by the creatures of the earth.
*You were above scenery, and guarded, beside
an oak, heavy with ivy, an inky depth.*

4
The trees were insubstantial, down below,
as if flattened, like an image in a book
and you leaned over it, forging memories.
There was a tilting wedge of light – some alloy
poles propped against a cloud – yet to be used.
How real you seemed, your mask stitched over
the shadows of an evergreen. I stood below you,
pasted over a flooded field, a hedge,
and the lit up windows of the abbey church.


5
You walked up to the wall and stretched,
on tip-toes, to the window. You stooped over the weir.
Your skin took on a filmy glow –
with the willow bough – above the water.
You turned your face to me, *"there's something here,"*
and in that umbellic light – balanced on its stalks –
I saw you leaning over something lost
you could not name, as if it was not there.

# A Southampton Stone Circle

## 1 Abstraction

It is all interpretation, when abstracted –
the ground, the stone, the fallen tree –
in which connections still remain,
as subtext, where distinctions raise
their ghostly ramparts over me.
The ovoid form drawn on the hill,
behind your house, which we have traced
through gardens – a rucked lawn, a border –
is an abstract image of the egg
which holds the passion, preserving it.


## 2 Tradition

The light on the far field, a row of yews,
and cow parsley, have risen into me.
I see the things you did not say
in ditch or bank, or buried stone,
where something unremembered is,
a love, or something else unknown.
"...it becomes even conscious
of itself," you said. *But you encoded it, in this.*

## 3  The Line

The line which tells the truth remains
obscured from us – a labyrinth
of names and pastures, misaligned,
and a cornucopia of broken things. Between
what we see and what we might deduce,
there is this essence of the self. A stone
tilted into the romance of its placing.
Children walk the circle – a hidden garden
in the air above the budded apple tree –
and they are told what childhood is.


## 4  Meaning

It is all geometry, this consciousness –
signs without meanings, magically
transforming us – though we don't know
of any context for the line
that draws the landscape into us.
I walk the path which gives itself
to you and all that you have held.
O brightening glance, it does not seek
to change its love, in knowing it.

**Part Four: The Source**

# Ha Ha

*"...a raid on the inarticulate..."*

*One: In Astoria*

We began at sunrise – a half light over the fields – on the slope behind the church. We splashed through flooded pastures to the ford, seeing, in perspective, how the church seemed to rise on the back of the barrow, long and steep. The hill did not tip its light over us, nor did the cow parsley – not cupping any meaning – place its light, nor any light, into our eyes. *Do not take these words at face value, they also sway on stilts, dangerously, invisibly.*

1
About the bunker, an aspen ring.
An abandoned curtilage or enclosure;
some discrete shrine, overrun or remaindered.
We encountered it as *image*, a complex
of meanings – a brute reorganisation
of some occluded principle, a mystery.
There was a tiny room, fire blackened,
and a passage under concrete with
a latched gate into the furnace. Old
graffiti – "ALL FUCKED UP" – signed, *Smiffy*.
A split bag, a sentencing, her clothes
twisted amongst the debris – cotton
print, a flowering – and damp bricks.
We tidied a corner and waited.

2
Above ground, a quivering of leaves – reflected
in the ditch – played host to memories.
Lost moments were remembered then because
an almost abstract shape, a subtlety,

shifted as it had before – releasing
a reek of *things* – an urge, an agreement.
She looked at me and I gave in,
saying "no" and turning away – as before –
with a joke designed to distance her.
She was wakeful, in the silence then, as if
aware of space, of a hollowness, below me.
"*My heart is closed*," I said. A fallen tree
had blocked the path. She looked at it, victorious.

3
*An infill of bricks in the shaft. Some
calamitous event had caved it in.*
It was no longer historical, the bunker,
in being abandoned. It had fallen
out of narrative, the raised ideal, and lost its edge.
A vallum flung about an emptiness,
yoked to Nato. A tank shed constructed
in the interior, close to an anxiety.
*Concrete.* A retaining wall, still in place,
though the ground had gone from under it.
An image of a commonwealth denied
in borders and centres, a fused grove –
or something else administered, a consciousness –
that vanished when you looked at it.

*Two: Muster Point*

A faint shining of something lost in the distance, a memory placed up ahead. Guarded fortress. Identity on a ridge. *Mons Badonicus*. Here, the Dorset Clubmen drew a line. *Home Guard*. The Romance of Arthur. *'poor silly creatures'*. Local colours – raised against a Parliament – on insubstantial ground. *I am placed in you like this*. What we have of self negation, what we lose in a glance, can be realised. Kicking in, such hidden matter, *our very culture*, lifts this landscape into light, where you materialise, raising me with your smile.

*1 Badbury Rings*

It is the proud boast of the county (backdated).

> A medal in a glass case.
> A local landmark.
> *A shrine.*

An earlier one is hidden in the ground –
earlier and so 'innocent' – pre-dating brutality, the fall.

A symbol of the earth – a sacrificial enclosure –

it leaves a sour after taste.

> *A spiral of rooks*

in the distance

> *to represent the self.*

We meet in the car park, below the earthen walls.

On the skyline, an empty crown. An emblem.

A frame, since filled in with earth.
*A cavity left by a name that has gone.*

    An authority.

A discontinued line, the diction of governance.

Cast in this mould, a buried magnet
drawing soil into the typical pattern. *Iron Age.*

In plan, the funerary brooch of a king, regularised, the pin gone.

A collar. A yoke. A distant war.

A pronouncement or policy statement leading to
a jubilee – old values, revived or reinvented – an implied border.
*Meaning expressed as 'that which limits'.* Our hospitality.

    A source, always set back.
    Found in antiquity, the binding name.


## 2  Tarrant Rushton

We found the airfield she had said was "half-remembered."
*A triangular plan.*
A giant letter A.
A system of runways, dug up.

"Alpha," she said, turning from the text, "it *is* an A!"

A magical symbol, the image –
an order of events –
implying a journey we might take into the alphabet.

We walked to the runway from the barrow of the pilot.
The mechanics of the faith; an obsolete doctrine;
a symbol to imagine systems by. *An ideal thing.*

A bunker or circular mound, *freshly ploughed.*

Stronghold of bomber command.
Muster point.
Blockhouse of earth, this circular earthwork.
A defence against death. Hidden
and warmed by the sun,

a castle with glass walls. A line of descent
along the Roman road.

Cursus laid upon cursus – an outline ahead.

Where paths cross, the pattern of runways
mirroring the layout of the Roman roads
around the fort.

A discrete inheritance or ideogram
of the warrior caste. *Shamanic flight.*

The power of the ritual overcomes fear,
repressing it into the landscape.
*A glider towed along the runway.*

D-Day, an act of faith. The towrope, a doctrine.

A system of runways – a ghost under furrows.

In this ground; bronze age warriors;
a crashed Halifax bomber; an eye-glass;
the shadow of a calf-skin cap; *bone goggles –*

a hex, a watermark, a geometry
last spoken by Enoch. *Mute hieroglyph.*

*Ancestral badge.* The continuity
of arrivals and departures.


## 3  Her Ideas

Away from shadows and the letter 'A', she picked at flowers,
taking them apart, "as if stripping skin."
*To be clothed only in the spirit.*

There was a succession of men, she said – reaching right back into
Antiquity – a series of betrayals resulting in
The Tradition, our culture, the way we live.
Bladdud, Artorius, then Horsa.

And all the soldiers they could find
packed into a wicker horse with wings
and towed out amongst Flak
and other fiery demons.

Men enjoy war, she said. Apollo over the earth –
rapine sunlight – the words of the poet
also a part of the slaughter.

*She was gutted. Our History is her Anatomy.*
A flag or insignia.

*Horsa not towed behind, but released into futurity.*

Men are *naturally* invasive.
And archaeology – it's just the same.

She was in her anger, as if I might describe
her culture and cartography, going deeper into her body
than she had preferred,
to feel the truth of what it was that lingered there –
"like faded text," I said –
or know the tenderness of flesh, with her eclipsing it again.

*The tenderness of flesh?*

Such comfort.

A lyric of mine in her skin –
or the light of her skin –
in her heart –
or a knowledge, or the light of that –
and her gentleness, her strength, as it was.

*How we might take control of our lives.*

We stood above the gate,
unaware of our selves:
harmed and unharmed,
freed and bound,
empowered and disempowered.

*Lighter than air, an idea of fields.*

There was an antlered oak

dying in the view –

        an insubstantial giant

becoming ill-defined

    like an aerial dissolving

in fog – a self, decaying –

    overwhelmed by the broadcast.

*Too many perspectives.*

Cernunnos of the matter in hand –

numinous with memory –

letting go of everything.

Death beyond language. Things set free

from the prison of names.
*A metamorphosis.* The end of perspective.

Within us all, a vanishing point
reversed – a universe
no-one has described,

that moment of being –

the lived image.

*Three: The Giant*

We'd imagined the past we would walk to in time. It was our invention, there – on that cusp of slope – on that believable ground. I watched you pause and visualise. *False histories.* It has been so long since I last sensed the ancient eclipse of a tree by my myth of it. I waited, calling up a legion of dead voices from the very features that my feet had crushed – *that* leaf litter, *those* blades of grass – a democratic chorus, something reassuring. You stood in the deep nostalgia of adolescence – those fleshy leaves – the moist green pits of summer. *A view opened up over giant and hedgerow...*

I
It's the way you can't see him close up.

Oblique incline. Something glimpsed over
the tops of the trees.

  You have to turn your back
and walk away to know him.

  Ethereal
memory of something touched, how you

    thrilled me,

despite illness, rejection – that clear light
over the summit.

  Our losses
appeared in him –
    distanced and idealised –

within the glassy turf.

From the fence you can see his feet.

2
He was watching over your shoulder, his cock
pressed into your thigh. The bastard
doesn't give up. For him our distances contain
an intimacy – something you'd thought
was lost. That holy other reclines

on his hill, watching us, in his come-
and-get-me pose, saying, "Marry me or
I'll kill you." The ritual includes
a locked church – its silences –
and you slit open, demanding attention.

3
He is suspended from the sky by light.
The hill is braced by scaffolding.
There is nothing of nature, the land is *made*:
he keeps the ground from falling into place.
Near Cerne Park we saw him prise

the landscape from our sense of self.
Without him there we'd never have survived
the weight of gravity and history
to peer beneath the lip of turf to see
beyond legend, into innocence.

4
Ragamuffin god? Unholy emperor? Shallow tyrant?
What is to be done with you now?
They stare for a while, fascinated, and turn away
leaving you fixed in place
by their mything of themselves.

What are these truths they tell you of
but cowardice? At the moment of release

they run back into childishness
to scratch a shallow outline in the place
of something brave in them they had denied.

5
We climbed towards Cerne Park to find
a place that we could see him from
and found the wider brilliances
of landscapes hanging from the sky. Turfed
elevation trodden into myth, the

endless ridged maze of the slope. We paused
for photographs, dwarfing the giant, and looked
beyond the view carelessly – laughing
and displaced – like passengers,
lit up and moving.

6
"Queen of the May, caught up in incest and starved
into a thin blossom, you have held a hand
in the underworld and been controlling –
only allowing the engines
to briefly come alive. Bring us spring
as it is, not as it is dreamed,
that we might hold the hand of some lost self
we loved but were afraid of and denied."

In that instant of speech he ignited
and staggered on the hill, laughing.

7
You lifted the lid of the tomb so I could see
the machinery, intact – the engines called
*Reliant* and *Victory* – the greasy undersides of hills,

thick with asbestos. I pulled
the lever marked 'Plateaux' and felt the platform rise

over thatch and shambles, the bus stop.

The rampart was still working (you seemed surprised)
and we kicked the engine over for a joke
and place just rumbled into life, heavily polluting,
and we ran – laughing – from what we'd started.

8
And we crept back into the engine room –
pulled clear the oily rags, old overalls – seeking
the red button that would switch place off.
We could feel the pressure falling. There was a clunk and a
shudder, and you pulled hard on the lever – greasing it –

and we climbed into the pastoral we'd made,
sealing the cast iron trapdoor in the soil, and covering it over,
and we said farewell to that old milky giant
who dozed within the myth
and you dabbed grease on my nose.

    "Ha ha", was all you said.

*Four: Wee Willy*

A cloud turning over a knoll to the west, the form above reflecting that below. An identification. A pretence of similarity. A process of comparison. Eye to eye. Mouth to mouth. Heart to heart. Hand to hand. *No actual similarity existed.* She chalked a Smiley face onto the wall. A matchstick body and some limbs, a cock and balls. "Wee Willy," she said, "my handsome." A pristine sign or *demon* then, up for anything, or so the symbol might predict, concealing what it once described.

An image of her in the lane.
An hour waiting
by the phone box.

The wet bench
carved with names, inky leaves.

I walked through fog to the lay-by
beneath
colossal legs rising from
the melancholy lustre of the trees.

*Sticky underfoot.*
Her mobile off.

Near the car park, a bed of crushed stalks;
vomit on the nettles
where she lowered her pulse
into the earth, sleeping it off?

"I spoke to her earlier and she seemed
okay." I think that's what I said.

*"The fucking bitch."*

She rose from sleep beneath a hedge,
drawing an arc
with her arm
over steeped trees,
enclosing them.

Way off over the heights
nodding donkeys
worked the interior,
hauling a hill.

We saw a landscape emerging
from the fog. An object of the mind –
traditional in form – an image renewed
by scouring. It was
tilted from the hammering it took (5° off).

Think *local* and imagine this;

a distinct region;
a meaningful history;
a culture that reflects upon itself;
Justice; Reason;
all 'abstract stuff' that represents
a private dilemma or
*the moral dimension*
as it relates to feelings.

A new technology installed
on ancient battlefields;
the progress of enclosure;
not power dispersed but
power disguised; an abdication,
this absence of meaning,
the poor getting poorer;

a state of governance then,
a metaphor of Unity?

*Contested signs.*

A monument, "a rich hoard of symbols";
a new consciousness
we may not get to like.

She led me along

a linear ditch –

"a weld mark

on a line of stress" –

and pointed to

a mast raised

on a distant hill –

an image of her self –

with everything

hanging on

its broadcast.

www.ingramcontent.com/pod-product-compliance
Lightning Source LLC
Chambersburg PA
CBHW021327190426
43193CB00039B/445